MAKE A MEAL OF CHEESE

Produced by the Cheese Information Service,
who would like to thank the following for their co-operation
in supplying accessories for use in the photographs:
General Trading Company (Mayfair) Ltd,
144 Sloane Street, London SW1.

Casa Pupo, 56 Pimlico Road, London SW1.

Elizabeth David Ltd, 46 Bourne Street, London SW1.

Robert Jackson & Co Ltd, 172 Piccadilly, London W1.

Recipes suggested, tested and prepared for photography by:
Dairy Produce Advisory Service, Milk Marketing Board,
Thames Ditton, Surrey.

Photographs by Roger Tuff.

Printed in England by Sir Joseph Causton & Sons Ltd,
London and Eastleigh.

Index to Recipes

MAKE A MEAL OF CHEESE

Cheese is one of our best and most economical protein foods. It is extremely versatile and can be eaten at any time of day as a main meal or a snack, cooked or uncooked. It is easily digestible and comes in so many different types and flavours, there is a variety to suit the tastes of all age groups and palates.

Cheese can be grated for sauces, salads, for sprinkling on soup, for scones and pastry, or for grilling to make a hot snack. It can be cubed for salads, speared on cocktail sticks with pineapple, gherkin, chopped fruit and vegetables, or to make a tasty pie or pastry filling. A hunk of cheese is delicious with fruit or apple pie, gingerbread or fruit cake, or of course just on its own.

This book is designed to give you some ideas for using cheese in any of your meals, and particularly, lots of ways of cooking with cheese. All the cheese referred to in the recipes is of the hard-pressed type, usually Cheddar, because this variety is most suitable for use in cooked dishes. There are literally hundreds of different types, and the cheese board containing a wide selection makes a superb end to a meal.

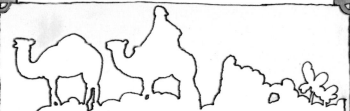

History of cheese

Cheese is known to have been eaten by the Greeks, Romans and Jews over two thousand years ago. No one knows for sure how it was discovered but, according to one legend, cheese was first found accidentally by nomadic Arab tribesmen in the desert. These tribes carried with them ewes' milk in a bag made from a dried sheep's stomach. When the bag was opened, it was found to contain curds and whey. The heat of the sun had turned the milk sour as the sheep's stomach contained a little rennin, which had a curdling effect on the milk and had made a simple form of cheese.

Since then, cheese has come a long way. Cheeses were traditionally made in country farmhouses. Different soil, grass, climate and maturity resulted in subtle differences in the flavours of each of the cheeses. However, before the old crafts were forgotten, the famous regional cheeses were successfully reproduced in modern creameries.

Some farmhouse cheese is still made, but this represents a very small amount of,the cheese we consume. Cheeses today have all the flavour produced by the craftsmen and, in addition, a high standard of hygienic production.

A healthy family

We probably don't realise as we bite into a piece of cheese, the amount of milk it contains. Cheese is one of the finest natural foods. It is, in fact, the oldest way of preserving and concentrating the goodness of milk, and so it has excellent nutritional value.

Eight pints of fresh milk are needed to make one pound of Cheddar cheese. Cheese is one of our best and most economical sources of protein and calcium, thus making it a very important body-building food. It is essential for growth and repair of our body tissues. Whatever the age group, cheese has an important part to play in the well-balanced healthy diet. One ounce of cheese contains as much protein as one and a half ounces of raw stewing steak. Cheese has more protein, ounce for ounce, than raw meat, fish or eggs. It is also rich in calcium and contains useful amounts of Vitamins A and D. So it's easy to see that cheese is very good value for money.

Cheese is especially important for children, and both young children and babies love the taste, so it can be easily introduced into their diet at an early age. Old people also find cheese ideal. That old wives' tale about indigestibility just isn't true. It's very easy to eat and digest.

Shopping and budgeting

Hard cheese, like Cheddar, is available either cut from a whole cheese in its traditional form, that is shaped like a barrel and wrapped in muslin, and coated with wax, or cut from a rindless rectangular block and either wrapped in film or waxed paper or in a vacuum pack. So whether you have two or more to cook for, or whether you live alone, cheese is very economical as you can always buy it in whatever amounts you want, never mind how little, and there's no waste.

If you prefer to shop in larger quantities, remember cheese will keep for a week or two.

Many grocers are now selling cheese in pre-packed portions to ensure that it reaches you in excellent condition, and cheese packed in this way will often keep longer.

Cheese storage

One advantage of cheese is its keeping qualities. The best way to store cheese is to wrap it loosely in a polythene bag, greaseproof paper or foil, or in a covered dish to prevent it from becoming dry. If the cheese has been purchased in a pre-packed container, it is advisable to remove the cheese after opening each pack, and then store in the same way. If, when you remove the wrapping, the surface of the cheese is wet, allow it to dry naturally before eating.

Keep your cheese in a cool larder or in a refrigerator and take it out an hour before serving to bring it to room temperature to allow the full flavour to return.

For convenience, grate any dry or left-over cheese and keep it in an air-tight container in a cool place. It will keep for several weeks and it is then handy for cooking or for flavourings and garnishes.

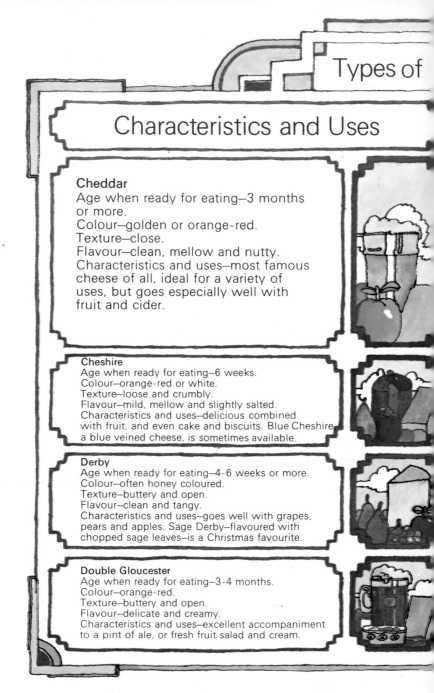

Characteristics and Uses

Cheddar
Age when ready for eating—3 months or more.
Colour—golden or orange-red.
Texture—close.
Flavour—clean, mellow and nutty.
Characteristics and uses—most famous cheese of all, ideal for a variety of uses, but goes especially well with fruit and cider.

Cheshire
Age when ready for eating—6 weeks.
Colour—orange-red or white.
Texture—loose and crumbly.
Flavour—mild, mellow and slightly salted.
Characteristics and uses—delicious combined with fruit, and even cake and biscuits. Blue Cheshire, a blue veined cheese, is sometimes available.

Derby
Age when ready for eating—4-6 weeks or more.
Colour—often honey coloured.
Texture—buttery and open.
Flavour—clean and tangy.
Characteristics and uses—goes well with grapes, pears and apples. Sage Derby—flavoured with chopped sage leaves—is a Christmas favourite.

Double Gloucester
Age when ready for eating—3-4 months.
Colour—orange-red.
Texture—buttery and open.
Flavour—delicate and creamy.
Characteristics and uses—excellent accompaniment to a pint of ale, or fresh fruit salad and cream.

Cheeses

Characteristics and Uses

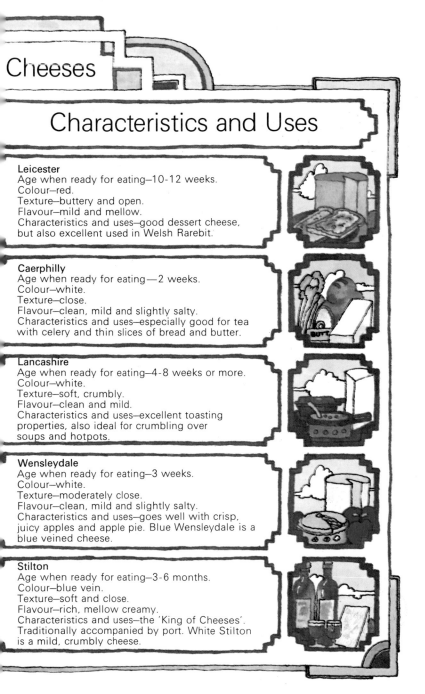

Leicester
Age when ready for eating—10-12 weeks.
Colour—red.
Texture—buttery and open.
Flavour—mild and mellow.
Characteristics and uses—good dessert cheese,
but also excellent used in Welsh Rarebit.

Caerphilly
Age when ready for eating—2 weeks.
Colour—white.
Texture—close.
Flavour—clean, mild and slightly salty.
Characteristics and uses—especially good for tea
with celery and thin slices of bread and butter.

Lancashire
Age when ready for eating—4-8 weeks or more.
Colour—white.
Texture—soft, crumbly.
Flavour—clean and mild.
Characteristics and uses—excellent toasting
properties, also ideal for crumbling over
soups and hotpots.

Wensleydale
Age when ready for eating—3 weeks.
Colour—white.
Texture—moderately close.
Flavour—clean, mild and slightly salty.
Characteristics and uses—goes well with crisp,
juicy apples and apple pie. Blue Wensleydale is a
blue veined cheese.

Stilton
Age when ready for eating—3-6 months.
Colour—blue vein.
Texture—soft and close.
Flavour—rich, mellow creamy.
Characteristics and uses—the 'King of Cheeses'.
Traditionally accompanied by port. White Stilton
is a mild, crumbly cheese.

1 Cheddar
2 Cheshire
3 Stilton
4 Caerphilly
5 Double Gloucester
6 Leicester
7 Wensleydale
8 Lancashire
9 Derby
10 Dunlop

The varieties of traditional cheese

Cheese-making is a well established tradition throughout the British Isles, and over the years a number of famous territorial varieties have grown up. Many of them are still made in the areas where they originated, but the most important cheese, Cheddar, is now produced in many different centres as the map shows.

Cheddar was first made near the Cheddar Gorge some 400 years ago, and is now the most popular cheese available. For many generations the Ploughman's Lunch—cheese, butter, bread and ale has been the pride of the country inn.

Cheshire was first produced in the twelfth century, and is the oldest of all traditional cheeses.

The rare Blue Cheshire is one of the most superb blue cheeses in the world and, with its rich and creamy taste, is well worth shopping for.

Stilton. Seventeen gallons of milk go into each prime Stilton. The characteristic blue veining and tangy flavour is formed by piercing the cheese with stainless steel needles to allow the penetration of a penicillium mould, which is present in the air in the buildings in which Stilton is made. The best Stilton is made from summer milk, and it is at its best at Christmas.

Caerphilly, originally from Wales, is a favourite with the miners. No longer, however, is it made in the small mining area that gave it its name, but it still has its traditional cake-like shape, so designed to enable miners working in the pits to cut it in easily-held wedges for lunch.

Double Gloucester. This is a traditional West Country cheese and at one time there was a single and a double, differing in age and thickness, but only Double Gloucester is available now.

Leicester. Locals say it makes the best Welsh Rarebit in the world, and they mean real Welsh Rarebit—made with mustard, beer, butter and eggs, and poured over the toast.

Wensleydale was originally made by the monks of Jervaulx Abbey. In the North, they're very partial to it with a slice of apple pie, and it goes well with a crisp, juicy apple.

Lancashire was once a staple food with the mill workers of the cotton towns. It is one of the best cooking cheeses in the world and especially good for soups and sauces. Lancastrians crumble it over Lancashire Hotpot for extra tang and flavour.

Derby is more rare than most. The Sage Derby, flavoured with chopped sage leaves, is a rare but particularly attractive cheese and is a traditional Christmas favourite.

Dunlop and Orkney. Dunlop is a traditionally mellow Scottish cheese which is now produced mainly in the islands of Arran and Islay. Orkney has a similar texture which is slightly softer than Cheddar.

Cooking with cheese

Cheese is excellent for cooking with, and none of its nutritional value is lost. However, it should never be overcooked; it only needs to be melted to impart its full flavour to the other ingredients, so always cook cheese slowly over a low heat.

Hints and ideas

Store a quantity of grated Cheddar cheese in a covered container in the refrigerator. It is then always ready for instant use. Sprinkle into soups and stews. Add to flans, pies and sauces.

4 level tablespoons of dry, grated cheese weigh approximately one ounce.

Use 2 oz for a hurried lunch.

Use 4 oz for a cheese sauce.

Use 8 oz for a luxury-looking, yet budget dish when friends come for a meal.

Dice it to serve at a party.

Slice it for sandwiches.

Grate it for cooking.

Blend it for a sauce.

Bake it for a hot meal.

Grill it for a quick snack.

Snacks

One of cheese's great virtues is its ease of preparation. Snacks with cheese are quick and simple and even if you don't have time to cook, tuck into a generous hunk of cheese; it's both delicious and nourishing.

If you don't have time to have a cooked breakfast, try a slice of cheese with your toast. With morning coffee, try crumbled cheese on a sweet buttered digestive biscuit.

Replace that starchy lunch box with this quick-to-prepare meal: chunks of cheese, soft fresh bread, crisp chicory, celery and firm tomatoes.

When the children come home hungry from school, give them a piece of cheese and an apple; also a speedy sweet for a busy day. This is the subject for a well-known phrase—
'An apple without cheese is like a kiss without a squeeze.'
Whatever time of day you eat it, cheese can turn a snack into a nutritious meal.

Breakfasts
Lack of time in the morning is sometimes the reason for having little or no breakfast. But, with a little forethought, preparation need not be a chore, and your family will start the day better equipped for both work and play.

A real breakfast quickie is to serve slices of cheese with croissants or slices of white and brown bread.

Starters
Cheese makes a good start to a meal. It can be a glamorous beginning to a grand dinner party or a hearty start to a family meal.

Desserts
Ever tried cheese with pears or dried fruit or oranges? The sweet and savoury flavour is most unusual and exciting!

Cheese sauce—how to make it and how to use it
Cheese sauce is generally used in one of four consistencies, each for different dishes. Each is made by the same simple method.

1 A thin pouring sauce:
 1 oz butter
 1 oz flour
 1½ pints milk
This sauce is the basis for soups.

2 A pouring sauce:
 1 oz butter
 1 oz flour
 1 pint milk
This is used where pasta or vegetables will be added to the sauce to form a dish such as macaroni cheese.

3 A coating sauce:
 1 oz butter
 1 oz flour
 ½ pint milk
This is used to cover fish, eggs, vegetables or meat.

4 A panada (binding sauce):
 1 oz butter
 1 oz flour
 ¼ pint milk
This is a very thick sauce and is the basis of soufflés.

In each case use 4-8 oz of Cheddar cheese (grated) to each pint of liquid.

STARTERS

Quick Tuna Mousse

Serves 4

1 (6½ oz) can tuna (drained)
2 eggs (beaten)
½ pint milk
4 oz Cheddar cheese (grated)
4 tablespoons mayonnaise
1 stick celery (finely chopped)
Salt and pepper
Lemon wedges
Parsley
Fingers of toast

1 Preheat oven—mark 2, 300°F.
2 Mash tuna in a basin, then add eggs, milk, cheese, mayonnaise, celery, salt and pepper. Mix thoroughly.
3 Place mixture into 4 buttered ovenproof dishes. Smooth tops.
4 Bake for approximately 40 minutes.
5 Serve hot, garnished with a lemon wedge and sprigs of parsley on each, with fingers of hot toast.

Tip: These may be served cold and are an ideal dish for a picnic, too!

Crunchy Stuffed Eggs

Serves 4

4 hard-boiled eggs
2 oz Cheddar cheese (finely grated)
1 oz salted peanuts (chopped)
1 tablespoon milk or fresh cream
Salt and pepper
1 lettuce
2 tomatoes (sliced)

1 Cut eggs in half lengthwise. Remove yolks and place in a basin. Add cheese, peanuts, milk, salt and pepper. Mix well together.
2 Pile mixture back into the egg cases. Serve on a bed of lettuce garnished with slices of tomato.

Cheese and Onion Soup

Serves 4

1 oz butter
2 onions (cut into rings)
2 sticks celery (chopped)
1 oz flour
1 pint milk
$\frac{1}{2}$ pint stock
Salt and pepper
Pinch of nutmeg
6 oz Cheddar cheese (grated)
2 slices bread
Parsley (chopped)

1 Melt the butter in a large saucepan. Lightly fry onion rings and chopped celery without browning.

2 Add flour and cook for 1-2 minutes. Gradually beat in the milk, stock and seasoning. Heat, whisking continuously, until the soup thickens. Simmer for 5 minutes.

3 Meanwhile, toast the bread on one side. Sprinkle 2 oz grated cheese on untoasted side. Grill until the cheese melts. Cut into small squares.

4 Remove soup from heat. Stir in remaining grated cheese. Pour into warmed soup bowls or a tureen and float toasted cheese on top. Serve.

Tomatoes Gervaise

Serves 4

4 large tomatoes
4 oz Cheddar cheese (finely grated)
1 oz cooked ham (finely chopped)
Salt and pepper

1 Cut a slice from the top of each tomato (rounded end). Using a teaspoon, remove the seeds of the tomatoes.

2 Place seeds and lids of tomatoes (chopped) in a bowl. Add cheese, ham, salt and pepper.

3 Fill the tomatoes with this mixture and place under a hot grill until cheese melts. Serve hot or cold.

Tip: These make an interesting vegetable to serve with grilled chops, too!

Fluffy Cheese Ramekins

Serves 6

1 oz butter
1 onion (finely chopped)
2 oz streaky bacon (chopped)
2 tomatoes (chopped)
2 oz mushrooms (chopped)
Salt and pepper
$2\frac{1}{2}$ fl oz milk
2 eggs (separated)
6 oz Cheddar cheese (grated)
Salt and pepper

1 Preheat oven—mark 5,375°F.

2 Melt the butter in a saucepan and gently fry the onion. Add bacon, tomatoes and mushrooms. Season well and place in 6 buttered ramekin dishes.

3 Place milk, egg yolks and cheese in a saucepan. Heat gently until cheese has melted.

4 Whisk egg whites until stiff. Fold carefully into the cheese mixture. Pour into the ramekin dishes.

5 Bake for 10-15 minutes until well risen and golden brown. Serve immediately.

Seafood au Gratin

Serves 6

1 lb potatoes (peeled)
3 oz butter
2 hard-boiled eggs (sliced)
2 tomatoes (sliced)
4 oz prawns
1 oz flour
Salt and pepper
$\frac{1}{2}$ pint milk
3 oz Cheddar cheese (grated)
Parsley

1 Preheat grill.

2 Cook potatoes in boiling salted water. Mash well and add 2 oz butter. Fork mixture into a border in 6 scallop shells or individual ovenproof dishes.

3 Place slices of hard-boiled egg and tomato in each 'nest'. Top with the prawns, reserving a few for decoration.

4 Place 1 oz butter, flour, salt, pepper and milk into a saucepan. Heat, whisking continuously, until the sauce thickens. Add most of the cheese and beat well. Pour sauce into the centre of the nests.

5 Sprinkle sauce with remaining cheese. Grill until golden. Garnish with prawns and parsley, serve hot.

Pot au Feu

Serves 4–6

1 (15 oz) can tomatoes
$\frac{1}{2}$ pint stock
2 carrots (chopped)
$\frac{1}{2}$ small white cabbage (shredded)
2 onions (chopped)
1 leek (chopped)
2 sticks celery (chopped)
1 small cauliflower (chopped)
Salt and pepper
4 oz Cheddar cheese (grated)
Parsley (chopped)

1 Place all the ingredients, except cheese and parsley, in a large saucepan. Simmer for 35-40 minutes.

2 Serve the soup sprinkled with cheese and parsley. Check seasoning.

Pot au Feu is a traditional French, country recipe which is continually allowed to simmer on the hot-plate, and so is immediately ready for serving when required.

It is suitable for serving as a meal in itself and can be varied by using different vegetables according to those in season.

22

Avocado Cocktail

Serves 4

1 avocado pear
4 oz Cheddar cheese (cubed)
3 sticks celery (chopped)
1 (5 fl oz) carton natural yogurt
2 tablespoons mayonnaise
Salt and pepper
1 rounded teaspoon curry powder
1 tomato (sliced)

1 Split avocado pear in half lengthwise. Discard the stone, then scoop out the flesh and roughly chop. Place in a basin. Add cheese and celery.

2 Blend together the natural yogurt, mayonnaise, seasoning and curry powder. Pour over chopped ingredients. Mix thoroughly.

3 Place mixture on to an oval platter, or in 4 individual dishes. Garnish with slices of tomato. Serve chilled.

Savoury Apple Starter

Serves 4

4 large dessert apples (washed)
1 tablespoon lemon juice
1 oz walnuts (chopped)
3 oz Cheddar cheese (grated)
2 tablespoons natural yogurt
1-2 sticks celery (chopped)
Lettuce
Watercress

1 Remove the core from each apple. Cut apples in half horizontally. Sprinkle lemon juice over cut surfaces.

2 Place walnuts, cheese, yogurt and celery into a basin. Mix thoroughly. Pile mixture into the cavities in apple halves.

3 Stand apple halves, cut side uppermost, on a bed of lettuce. Garnish with watercress and serve.

Cheese, Melon and Prawn Cocktail

Serves 6

1 small honeydew melon
$\frac{1}{2}$ lettuce (shredded)
8 oz Cheddar cheese (diced)
4 oz prawns
6 level tablespoons mayonnaise
4 tablespoons fresh cream
4 tablespoons tomato ketchup

1 Cut melon in half. Remove seeds, then cut flesh into cubes.

2 Divide the shredded lettuce between 6 deep cocktail glasses. Pile cheese, melon and prawns on top.

3 Blend together the mayonnaise, fresh cream and tomato ketchup. Spoon this sauce over the cocktail. Serve chilled.

Tip: Shredded white cabbage may be used instead of lettuce for a more crunchy cocktail.

Cheese Roundabouts

Serves 4

1 (7½ oz) packet frozen puff pastry (thawed)
6 oz Cheddar cheese
1 teaspoon made mustard
4 slices cooked ham
1 egg (beaten)
1 lettuce
1 tomato (quartered)

1 Preheat oven—mark 6, 400°F.

2 Roll out puff pastry to a rectangle of approximately 12 inches by 6 inches. Cut into 4 strips measuring 3 inches by 6 inches.

3 Cut the cheese into blocks 3 inches long and approximately 1 inch wide.

4 Place a slice of ham on each strip of pastry. Spread with mustard and place a block of cheese on top. Brush edges of pastry, then roll up and seal firmly.

5 Place on a dampened baking tray and brush with beaten egg.

6 Bake for 10-15 minutes until golden brown.

7 Serve cold on a bed of lettuce, garnished with tomato wedges.

Tip: These are ideal for snack meals and picnics, too!

MAIN MEALS

1. Crispy Medley Bake—Page 43
2. Cheese and Onion Roly Poly—Page 39
3. Cheese Kebabs—Page 43

Cod Timbale

Serves 4

1 lb potatoes (peeled)
Water
3 oz butter
4 oz Cheddar cheese (grated)
Salt and pepper
1 oz browned breadcrumbs
1 oz plain flour
$\frac{1}{2}$ pint milk
8 oz cod (cooked and flaked)
1 tablespoon parsley (chopped)
1 lemon (sliced)

1 Preheat oven—mark 5, 375°F.

2 Boil potatoes until soft. Drain and mash well.

3 Melt 2 oz butter in a saucepan. Add potatoes, cheese, salt and pepper. Beat well together.

4 Butter a $1\frac{1}{2}$-pint pudding basin. Sprinkle browned breadcrumbs inside to coat. Line basin with potato mixture, reserving about a third for the top.

5 Place remaining butter, flour, milk, salt and pepper in a saucepan. Heat, whisking continuously, until the sauce thickens. Add flaked fish and parsley. Pour into prepared mould.

6 Place remaining potato mixture on top to completely cover the basin.

7 Bake for 30-40 minutes. Allow to cool slightly, then turn out. Serve hot or cold, garnished with lemon slices.

Tip: When boiling potatoes for this recipe, place the cod on a heatproof plate above the saucepan, to steam. This saves gas or electricity.

Cheese and Ham Pie

Serves 6–8

1 lb plain flour
2 teaspoons salt
4 oz lard
$7\frac{1}{2}$ fl oz milk
8 oz cooked ham (diced)
6 oz Cheddar cheese (diced)
1 large onion (chopped)
Salt and pepper
4 hard-boiled eggs
1 egg (beaten)

1 Preheat oven—mark 4, 350°F.

2 Sieve together flour and salt on to a piece of greaseproof paper. Melt lard in a saucepan, add milk. Boil, then add sieved flour. Beat quickly, with a wooden spoon, to mix thoroughly. Turn out on to a floured board and knead the pastry well. Use while still warm.

3 Mould two-thirds of pastry into a 7-inch cake tin (preferably the loose-bottomed variety). Roll out remainder to a circle of about 8-inch diameter for the lid.

4 Place ham, grated cheese, onion, salt and pepper into a bowl. Mix well, then place in the prepared cake tin, leaving 4 hollows for hard-boiled eggs. Place eggs in position.

5 Place lid on pie, seal with beaten egg. Brush surface with beaten egg and decorate with pastry leaves.

6 Bake for 1-1$\frac{1}{4}$ hours, covering with greaseproof paper, if necessary, until golden brown. Serve hot or cold.

Tip: This is an economical pie which is delicious served hot or cold.

As a reminder of where the hard-boiled eggs are positioned within the pie, pastry leaves can be placed over the eggs to act as a guide for cutting.

Italian Pasta

Serves 4

3 oz spaghetti or vermicelli
Salt
Water
2 oz butter
2 large onions (thinly sliced)
4 oz streaky bacon (chopped)
1 oz plain flour
$\frac{1}{2}$ pint milk
Pepper
6 oz Cheddar cheese (grated)
1 teaspoon mixed herbs
2 tomatoes (skinned and chopped)
1 oz potato crisps (crushed)

1 Preheat grill.

2 Cook spaghetti in boiling salted water for 10-12 minutes. Drain.

3 Melt 1 oz butter in a frying pan, then fry onions and bacon, until cooked.

4 Place remaining butter, flour, milk, salt and pepper in a saucepan. Heat, whisking continuously, until the sauce thickens. Beat in 4 oz grated cheese and mixed herbs.

5 Combine cooked spaghetti, cheese sauce, tomatoes, onions and bacon. Place in a greased, ovenproof dish. Sprinkle with remaining cheese and crisps. Place under hot grill to brown. Serve hot.

Cheese Fondue

Serves 6

$\frac{1}{2}$ oz butter
$\frac{1}{2}$ pint cider or dry white wine
12 oz Cheddar cheese (grated)
1 level tablespoon cornflour
Black pepper
2 tablespoons Kirsch (optional)
1 crusty French loaf (cut into small cubes)

1 Place butter, cider, grated cheese, cornflour, pepper and Kirsch into a fondue dish, flameproof casserole or saucepan. Stir over a gentle heat until the fondue is smooth.

2 Keep warm. Serve by dipping cubes of French bread, on long-handled forks, into the fondue.

Tip: Fondues are great fun to serve when guests come for a meal. They originate from Switzerland where they serve a fondue on high days and holidays. Try serving a fondue at your next party, instead of a dip. Use long-handled forks or skewers for spearing bread.

Pancake Layer

Serves 4

4 oz plain flour
Pinch of salt
1 egg
2 oz butter (melted)
$\frac{1}{2}$ pint milk
6 oz Cheddar cheese (finely grated)
1 teaspoon Worcestershire sauce
2 tablespoons tomato purée
1 (5 fl oz) carton natural yogurt

1 Preheat oven—mark 4, 350°F.

2 Sieve flour and salt together into a bowl. Add egg, $\frac{1}{2}$ oz melted butter and a little milk. Beat to make a smooth batter. Stir in remaining milk.

3 Use remaining melted butter to brush the pancake pan. Fry tablespoonfuls of batter to make 8 pancakes. Keep hot.

4 Place 4 oz grated cheese, Worcestershire sauce, tomato purée and natural yogurt into a basin.
Mix thoroughly.

5 Spread cheese filling on to each pancake, stack on top of one another, in a shallow ovenproof dish, finishing with a pancake on top. Sprinkle remaining grated cheese over surface. Cover with aluminium foil.

6 Bake for 15-20 minutes to heat through. Remove foil. Serve hot.

Hawaiian Ham with Mustard Sauce

Serves 4

4 ham steaks
4 rings pineapple (drained)
4 oz Cheddar cheese (sliced)
1 oz butter
½ oz plain flour
1 teaspoon mustard powder
¼ pint milk
2 tablespoons vinegar
Salt and pepper
2 tomatoes (sliced)

1 Preheat grill.

2 Grill ham steaks for about 5-7 minutes on each side. Place in a shallow ovenproof dish. Top each with a ring of pineapple, then a slice of cheese. Return to grill to melt cheese. Keep hot.

3 Place butter, flour, mustard powder, milk, vinegar, salt and pepper in a saucepan. Heat, whisking continuously, until the sauce thickens.

4 Pour sauce over the ham and pineapple. Garnish with sliced tomatoes. Serve hot.

Cheesey Yorkshire Pudding

Serves 4

4 oz plain flour
Pinch of salt
1 egg
½ pint milk
1 oz butter
6 oz Cheddar cheese (cut into ¾-inch cubes)

1 Preheat oven—mark 7, 425°F.

2 Sieve together flour and salt into a basin. Make a well in the centre, add egg and stir in milk gradually. Beat until smooth.

3 Melt the butter in a small Yorkshire pudding tin. Toss in cheese cubes and pour in batter.

4 Bake until well risen, for 35-40 minutes. Serve immediately.

Cheesey Beef Carbonnade

Serves 4

$\frac{1}{2}$ oz butter
1 onion (chopped)
1 lb minced beef
1 oz plain flour
$\frac{1}{2}$ pint beer
8 oz small new potatoes (cooked)
2 oz button mushrooms
1 level tablespoon tomato purée
$\frac{1}{2}$ teaspoon Worcestershire sauce
Salt and pepper
2 oz Cheddar cheese (finely grated)
Parsley (chopped)

1 Melt butter in a frying pan. Add onion and minced beef, then fry gently for 5-10 minutes, until cooked.
2 Stir in flour, beer, new potatoes, button mushrooms, tomato purée, Worcestershire sauce, salt and pepper. Boil, then simmer for 25-30 minutes.
3 Serve on a hot platter, sprinkle with grated cheese and chopped parsley.

Tip: Delicious served with a tossed green salad. No more potatoes need be served.

Crusted Cheese Pie

Serves 4

2 oz butter
4 slices bread
1 teaspoon made mustard
6 oz Cheddar cheese (grated)
2 eggs (beaten)
$\frac{1}{2}$ pint milk
Salt and pepper
Watercress

1 Preheat oven—mark 4, 350°F.

2 Butter bread and spread with mustard. Cut each slice diagonally into 4.

3 Arrange layers of bread and cheese in a $1\frac{1}{2}$-pint ovenproof dish, finishing with a layer of cheese.

4 Beat together eggs, milk, salt and pepper. Pour over the bread. Leave aside for about 30 minutes.

5 Bake for $\frac{3}{4}$-1 hour, until set. Serve hot, garnished with watercress.

Haddock au Gratin

Serves 4

1 lb smoked haddock
$\frac{1}{4}$ pint milk
Salt and pepper
1 oz butter
2 hard-boiled eggs (chopped)
3 oz Cheddar cheese (grated)
1 oz fresh breadcrumbs
Parsley

1 Preheat oven—mark 4, 350°F.

2 Place smoked haddock in a shallow 2-pint ovenproof dish. Cover with milk, salt and pepper, then dot with butter.

3 Bake for 15-20 minutes until the fish is cooked.

4 Mix together hard-boiled eggs, grated cheese and breadcrumbs. Sprinkle on top of cooked fish. Return to oven to brown for 25 minutes. Serve hot, garnished with parsley.

Farmer's Sausagemeat Hotpot

Serves 4

1 lb sausagemeat
$\frac{1}{2}$ teaspoon mixed herbs
2 oz streaky bacon (chopped)
2 tomatoes (sliced)
Salt and pepper
1 cooking apple (peeled, cored and sliced)
4 oz Cheddar cheese
1 (4 serving) packet instant mashed potato

1 Preheat oven—mark 4, 350°F.

2 Line the base of a 3-pint ovenproof dish with sausagemeat. Sprinkle with mixed herbs.

3 Gently fry bacon in its own fat, until golden brown. Place in prepared dish, add tomato slices, salt, pepper and cooking apple. Sprinkle with grated cheese.

4 Top with mashed potato. Bake for 1 hour, until cooked through and golden brown.

Cheddar Curry

Serves 4

1 oz butter
1 onion (chopped)
1 oz plain flour
1–2 teaspoons curry powder
$\frac{1}{2}$ pint stock
Salt and pepper
2 level tablespoons sweet chutney
1 oz sultanas
6 oz Cheddar cheese (cubed)
4 oz long-grain rice (cooked)

1 Melt butter in a saucepan, add onion and fry until golden brown. Add flour and curry powder, stir over a gentle heat.

2 Gradually beat in the stock. Heat, whisking continuously, until the sauce thickens. Add salt, pepper, chutney, sultanas and cheese. Mix well.

3 Serve hot, on a shallow platter, surrounded by freshly cooked rice.

Tip: A very quick main meal—a useful standby using ingredients normally kept in the store cupboard.

Macaroni Mushroom Toss

Serves 4

6–8 oz macaroni
3 oz butter
8 oz button mushrooms (quartered)
2 onions (chopped)
1½ oz plain flour
¾ pint milk
Salt and pepper
½ teaspoon mustard
½ teaspoon Worcestershire sauce
8 oz Cheddar cheese (grated)

1 Preheat oven—mark 8, 450°F.

2 Cook macaroni, according to directions on the pack.

3 Melt 1½ oz butter in a saucepan. Add mushrooms and fry until lightly browned. Remove from pan.

4 Fry onions and cook until tender. Add mushrooms and macaroni.

5 Place remaining butter, flour, milk, salt, pepper, mustard and Worcestershire sauce in a saucepan. Heat, whisking continuously, until the sauce thickens. Stir in most of the cheese.

6 Add sauce to macaroni mixture. Place in a buttered 2-pint ovenproof dish. Sprinkle with remaining cheese. Bake for 10-15 minutes. Serve hot.

Cheese and Onion Roly Poly

Serves 4–6

8 oz self-raising flour
Pinch of salt
4 oz suet (shredded)
$2\frac{1}{2}$ fl oz milk
2 onions (chopped)
6 oz Cheddar cheese (grated)
1 egg (beaten)
2 tomatoes (sliced)
Watercress

1 Preheat oven—mark 6, 400°F.

2 Sieve together flour and salt into a bowl. Add suet and mix well. Bind together with milk.

3 Knead pastry lightly on a floured board, then roll out to a rectangle, approximately 15 inches by 12 inches.

4 Scatter chopped onion and grated cheese over the surface, leaving a margin of $\frac{1}{2}$ inch around each edge of pastry. Brush margin of pastry with beaten egg.

5 Roll up, Swiss roll fashion, and secure edges. Place on a flat baking sheet. Brush with beaten egg to glaze.

6 Bake for 35 minutes, until golden brown. Serve hot, garnished with sliced tomatoes and watercress.

Tip: Try forming the Roly Poly into a horseshoe shape for a change!

Quiche Lorraine

Serves 6–8

6 oz plain flour
Pinch of salt
2½ oz butter
1 egg yolk
Little water
6 oz streaky bacon (chopped)
2 eggs (beaten)
5 fl oz fresh cream
Pepper
6 oz Cheddar cheese (finely grated)
Parsley

1 Preheat oven—mark 7, 425°F.

2 Sieve together flour and salt into a bowl. Rub in the butter, until it resembles fine breadcrumbs. Add egg yolk and enough water to mix to a firm dough.

3 Roll out pastry and use to line an 8-inch flan ring or sandwich tin. Scatter bacon over the base.

4 Beat eggs, cream, salt, pepper and grated cheese together. Pour into prepared flan case. Bake for 10 minutes, then reduce oven temperature to mark 5, 375°F, and bake for a further 30-35 minutes. Serve hot or cold, garnished with parsley.

This is a true French Quiche Lorraine, filled with eggs, bacon, cheese and cream. Alternative ingredients may be included in the filling, such as onions, tomatoes, mushrooms, celery, sweetcorn or, in fact, any left-over cooked vegetables.

Quiche Lorraine is a marvellous way of using perishable foods before a holiday.

Ideal for a picnic.

Cider Baked Pork Chops

Serves 4

4 oz mushrooms (sliced)
2 cooking apples (peeled, cored and sliced)
1 onion (sliced)
Salt and pepper
4 pork chops
$\frac{1}{2}$ pint cider
2 oz browned breadcrumbs
4 oz Cheddar cheese (grated)
Watercress

1 Preheat oven—mark 6, 400°F.

2 Grease a 3-pint shallow ovenproof dish. Place mushrooms, apples and onions in base of dish. Season with salt and pepper.

3 Lay pork chops on the bed of vegetables. Cover with cider.

4 Mix together browned breadcrumbs and grated cheese. Sprinkle over the chops.

5 Bake for $1\frac{1}{4}$-$1\frac{1}{2}$ hours, until the chops are thoroughly cooked and the topping a golden colour. Garnish with watercress. Serve hot.

Cheese Kebabs

Serves 4

4 oz chipolata sausages
4 small onions
$\frac{1}{2}$ green pepper (cut into 8)
4 button mushrooms
4 tomatoes (halved)
6 oz Cheddar cheese (cubed)
Lettuce

1 Preheat grill.

2 Cut sausages in half. Grill, turning frequently, until thoroughly cooked and golden.

3 Blanch onions, pepper and mushrooms in boiling water for 1 minute, plunge immediately into cold water.

4 Arrange sausages, onions, pepper, mushrooms, tomatoes and cubed cheese attractively on skewers. Lay on a bed of lettuce. Serve cold.

A quick meal for a hot, summer's day!

Crispy Medley Bake

Serves 4

2 tomatoes (chopped)
4 tablespoons peas (cooked)
1 ($6\frac{1}{2}$ oz) can tuna (drained)
Salt and pepper
1 (7 oz) can condensed mushroom soup
$\frac{1}{4}$ pint milk
4 oz Cheddar cheese (grated)
$\frac{1}{2}$ oz potato crisps (crushed)
Parsley (chopped)

1 Preheat oven—mark 5, 375°F.

2 Place tomatoes, peas, tuna, salt and pepper in the base of a 1-pint ovenproof dish.

3 Blend soup with milk and pour over ingredients in the dish. Sprinkle with grated cheese and crushed crisps.

4 Bake for 20-25 minutes until golden brown. Sprinkle with chopped parsley. Serve hot.

Roast Chicken with Cheese and Peanut Stuffing

Serves 4–6

1 roasting chicken (approximately 3½ lb)
2 oz fresh breadcrumbs
4 oz Cheddar cheese (grated)
1 stick celery (finely chopped)
2 oz salted peanuts (chopped)
1 onion (finely chopped)
Salt and pepper
1 egg (beaten)
2 teaspoons lemon juice
2 oz butter (melted)

1 Preheat oven—mark 5, 375°F.

2 Prepare chicken for stuffing.

3 Mix together breadcrumbs, grated cheese, celery, salted peanuts, onion, salt and pepper in a basin. Bind ingredients with egg, lemon juice and a little melted butter.

4 Stuff chicken. Use any remaining to form into balls. Place chicken and stuffing balls on roasting tin.

5 Brush surface of chicken with remaining melted butter.

6 Bake for 1½-2 hours, depending upon the weight of chicken.

7 Serve hot, with a selection of vegetables and thickened gravy.

Potato Galette

Serves 4

1½ lb potatoes (peeled)
Salt
Water
2 oz butter
2 tablespoons milk
6 oz Cheddar cheese (grated)
8 oz onions (finely chopped)
1 egg (beaten)
Pepper
2 tomatoes (sliced)
4 oz streaky bacon (chopped)

1 Preheat oven—mark 6, 400°F.

2 Boil potatoes in boiling, salted water until soft.
Drain well, then mash with butter and milk.

3 Beat in 4 oz grated cheese, onions, beaten egg and
pepper. Turn into a shallow 9-inch ovenproof plate.
Mould to form a base.

4 Top potato mixture with slices of tomato, then
sprinkle chopped bacon on top. Cover with
remaining cheese. Bake for 20-30 minutes, until the
base is firm and the cheese melted. Serve hot.

Tip: A galette is a large pancake, normally served
in France. Instant mashed potatoes may be used to
save on preparation time.

Quick Cheese Pizza

Serves 4

6 oz self-raising flour
$\frac{1}{2}$ level teaspoon salt
2 oz butter
1 egg (beaten)
2 tablespoons milk
1 onion (sliced)
4 tomatoes (sliced)
Salt and pepper
1 teaspoon mixed herbs
6 oz Cheddar cheese (thinly sliced)
1 (2 oz) can anchovy fillets (drained)

1 Preheat oven—mark 7, 425°F.

2 Sieve together flour and salt into a bowl. Rub in 1 oz butter, then bind with beaten egg and milk to form a stiff dough.

3 Roll pastry to a circle of $\frac{1}{4}$-inch thickness. Place on a flat baking tray.

4 Melt remaining butter in a frying pan. Fry onion until soft. Place on pizza base. Top with tomato slices, salt, pepper, mixed herbs and sliced cheese.

5 Decorate with anchovies, lattice fashion. Bake for 30 minutes. Serve hot.

Vegetable Layer

Serves 4

1 lb potatoes (peeled and thinly sliced)
6 oz streaky bacon (chopped)
8 oz carrots (sliced)
2 oz mushrooms (sliced)
1 (4 oz) packet frozen sliced green beans
4 oz Cheddar cheese (finely grated)
2 eggs
½ pint milk
Salt and pepper
2 tomatoes (sliced)

1 Preheat oven—mark 4, 350°F.
2 Grease a 2-pint ovenproof pie dish. Place layers of potato, bacon, carrots, mushrooms, beans and grated cheese in the dish. Repeat until all ingredients are used, finishing with a layer of cheese.
3 Beat together eggs, milk, salt and pepper. Pour over ingredients in the dish.
4 Bake for 1-1½ hours until set and golden in colour. Serve hot, garnished with tomato slices.

Cheesey Lamb Chops

Serves 4

4 lamb chops
Salt and pepper
1 oz butter
3 oz Cheddar cheese (sliced)
2 tomatoes (sliced)
Watercress

1 Preheat grill.
2 Place chops on grill rack. Season with salt and pepper. Dot with butter. Grill on both sides until cooked.
3 Place a slice of cheese on each chop. Return to grill until cheese melts.
4 Place chops on a flat serving dish. Garnish with tomato slices and watercress. Serve hot.

Savoury Welsh Surprise

Serves 4

4 large leeks (or celery hearts or chicory)
Salt
Water
6 oz Cheddar cheese (cut into 4 fingers)
8 slices cooked ham
1 oz butter
1 oz plain flour
½ pint milk
Salt and pepper

1 Preheat oven—mark 5, 375°F.

2 Boil leeks in boiling salted water, until soft. Drain thoroughly. Roll each in a slice of ham. Roll fingers of cheese in slices of ham.

3 Arrange leek and cheese parcels in a shallow ovenproof dish.

4 Place butter, flour, milk, salt and pepper in a saucepan. Heat, whisking continuously, until the sauce thickens. Coat ingredients in dish with the sauce.

5 Bake for 30 minutes, until heated through and golden brown.

Tip: For a change, try substituting bananas for the cooked leeks. An exciting combination.

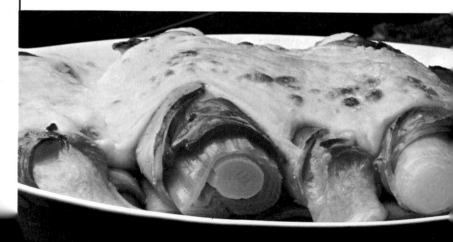

Fisherman's Mackerel

Serves 4

4 large mackerel
2 oz butter
1 small onion (finely chopped)
4 oz mushrooms (chopped)
2 oz fresh breadcrumbs
4 oz Cheddar cheese (grated)
Salt and pepper
1 lemon (sliced)
Parsley

1 Preheat oven—mark 4, 350°F.

2 Slit the mackerel along the side, clean out thoroughly, then rinse under running water.

3 Melt butter in a saucepan. Add onions, mushrooms, breadcrumbs, grated cheese, salt and pepper. Mix thoroughly and use to stuff mackerel.

4 Place fish in a shallow, buttered ovenproof dish. Cover with a lid or aluminium foil. Bake for 25-30 minutes, until thoroughly cooked and golden brown.

5 Garnish with lemon slices and parsley, then serve hot.

Tip: This stuffing is nice with herrings or poultry, too!

LIGHT LUNCHES AND SUPPER DISHES

1. Quick Chick Tartlets—Page 71
2. French Picnic Loaf—Page 63
3. Picnic Bars—Page 55

52

Packed lunch and picnics

Cheese is ideal for packed lunches and picnics. Sandwiches mean an instant picnic, but there's no need for them to be dull and monotonous. Try an exciting cheese spread and don't forget a hunk of cheese is delicious with a piece of fruit cake. Here are some simple but attractive ideas for sandwich fillings.

Grated Cheddar cheese, chopped celery, mayonnaise, watercress.

Sliced Cheddar cheese, mustard, tomato slices, watercress.

Grated Cheddar cheese and eating apple, pickle or chutney, lettuce.

Sliced Cheddar cheese, ham, mustard.

Sliced Cheddar cheese, rashers of crisply fried bacon, mustard.

Grated Cheddar cheese, mashed sardine, sliced cucumber.

Grated Cheddar cheese, chopped pineapple.

Grated Cheddar cheese, mayonnaise. (Also delicious toasted.)

Another must for a picnic is a Ploughman's Lunch.

This is easy to prepare and transport and so delicious to eat! Pack hunks of French bread or bread rolls, butter, tomatoes, lettuce, celery sticks, pickles, plenty of Cheddar cheese. Serve the Ploughman's Lunch with glasses of milk—kept chilled in a vacuum flask.

Nutty Cheese Loaf

Serves 4

6 oz streaky bacon
1 oz butter
6 oz peanuts (chopped)
1 onion (chopped)
2 oz fresh breadcrumbs
6 oz Cheddar cheese (grated)
1 tablespoon tomato purée
1 teaspoon mixed herbs
Salt and pepper
1 egg (beaten)
$\frac{1}{4}$ pint milk

1 Preheat oven—mark 5, 375°F.
2 Butter a 1 lb loaf tin and line with rashers of streaky bacon.
3 Melt the butter in a saucepan and add peanuts, onion, breadcrumbs, cheese, tomato purée, herbs, salt and pepper.
4 Add the egg and milk, then mix well together.
5 Turn into prepared tin and cover with greaseproof paper.
6 Bake for approximately 1 hour, until firm. Serve hot with vegetables or cold with a salad.

Cheese Cream Potatoes

Serves 4

1 (1 lb 3 oz) can new potatoes (drained)
4 oz Cheddar cheese (grated)
Salt and pepper
$7\frac{1}{2}$ fl oz fresh cream
Watercress

1 Preheat oven—mark 3, 325°F.
2 Place potatoes in a shallow ovenproof dish. Cover with cheese. Season with salt and pepper, then cover with cream.
3 Bake for 30 minutes. Garnish with watercress. Serve immediately.

Picnic Bars

Serves 4

1 (13 oz) packet frozen puff pastry (thawed)
1 large onion (finely chopped)
8 oz sausage meat
6 oz Cheddar cheese (grated)
2 tablespoons tomato purée
2 tablespoons fresh white breadcrumbs
1 egg (beaten)
Salt and pepper
Milk

1 Preheat oven—mark 6, 400°F.

2 Roll out the pastry into an oblong, approximately 14 inches by 10 inches. Place on a dampened baking tray.

3 Combine onion, sausage meat, cheese, tomato purée, breadcrumbs, egg, salt and pepper, then place in a strip down the centre of the pastry.

4 Dampen edges of pastry and seal together. Turn pastry over so that the join is underneath. Make diagonal cuts in pastry with a sharp knife. Brush with milk.

5 Bake for 35-40 minutes.

Serve the Picnic Bars hot or cold, cut into slices.

Cheese Hollow Loaf

Serves 6

1 small white crusty loaf
$\frac{1}{2}$ pint milk
2 oz butter
1 onion (chopped)
8 oz cooked meat (finely chopped)
1 tablespoon tomato purée
1 tablespoon parsley (chopped)
Salt and pepper
6 oz Cheddar cheese (grated)

1 Preheat oven—mark 5, 375°F.

2 Remove approximately 2 inches from the top of loaf. Scoop bread from inside of loaf and crumble half into breadcrumbs. Place in a basin, then add milk.

3 Melt butter in a saucepan and gently fry onion. Add meat, tomato purée, parsley, salt and pepper and cook for 5 minutes. Add breadcrumb mixture, then mix well together.

4 Place mixture in loaf and sprinkle with cheese. Replace 'lid' of loaf on top. Wrap loaf in aluminium foil.

5 Bake for 25-30 minutes. Serve hot or cold, cut into thick slices.

Let's have a salad

All you need to do is wash the fruit or vegetables, roughly chop them, add cheese and a salad dressing—your salad is then ready!

Salads are super on their own as a main meal or as an accompaniment to the main dish for lunch or dinner.

Cheese Salad

Serves 4–6

6 oz Cheddar cheese (diced)
2 carrots (grated)
2 red-skinned eating apples (chopped)
8 oz small white cabbage (finely shredded)
1 tablespoon lemon juice
2 oz raisins
1 oz walnuts (broken)
1 (5 fl oz) carton natural yogurt
Parsley (chopped)

1 Combine the cheese, carrots, apples, cabbage, lemon juice, raisins and walnuts together. Stir in yogurt and toss well.
2 Turn into a salad bowl and sprinkle with parsley. Serve with boiled new potatoes and whole tomatoes.

Here are some additional suggestions for attractive salads which can be made from either cubed or grated Cheddar cheese.

Shredded cabbage, diced apple and grated cheese tossed together with a little mayonnaise.

Left-over cooked vegetables and grated cheese served on lettuce with a French dressing.

Sliced tomato, sliced cucumber, sliced carrot served with cubed cheese.

Peeled and sliced oranges or grapefruit and grated cheese on a bed of lettuce.

Canned pineapple, drained, and grated cheese mixed with mayonnaise or yogurt and raisins.

Mixed fresh fruit and cubed cheese tossed in mayonnaise.

Grated cheese, grated carrot and chopped parsley tossed with cold macaroni or rice and a French dressing.

Chopped hard-boiled eggs, chopped celery and peanuts and cubed cheese tossed together and served on a bed of lettuce.

Sweetcorn, chopped tomatoes, chopped green pepper and cubed cheese, tossed together and served on a bed of lettuce.

Diced cold potato, chopped ham or chicken and grated cheese tossed together with yogurt.

Apart from the traditional salad comprising lettuce, cucumber and tomatoes, try serving rice-based salads, using cold cooked long-grain rice and any of the following flavourings:
Grated Cheddar cheese
Chopped cooked meats
Flaked cooked fish
Cooked mixed vegetables
Sliced cooked mushrooms
Grated carrot
Sultanas
Chopped dates
Chopped tomatoes
Chopped cucumber

Stuffed Peppers

Serves 4

4 firm green peppers
2 oz butter
2 rashers streaky bacon (chopped)
1 onion (finely chopped)
2 tomatoes (skinned and chopped)
2 oz long-grain rice (cooked)
$\frac{1}{4}$ teaspoon mixed herbs
Salt and pepper
4 oz Cheddar cheese (grated)

1 Preheat oven—mark 4, 350°F.

2 Cut a slice off the top of each pepper, then remove centre core and seeds. Stand peppers upright in an ovenproof dish.

3 Melt butter in a saucepan. Add bacon and onions, then fry gently until soft. Add tomatoes, rice, mixed herbs, salt and pepper. Pile mixture into pepper shells.

4 Top each with grated cheese.

5 Bake for 30-40 minutes, until peppers are tender. Serve hot.

Tip: This makes an ideal TV snack as it requires only a fork for eating.

Lunchtime Avocado

Serves 4

2 avocado pears
4 tablespoons cooking oil
2 tablespoons vinegar
Salt and pepper
Pinch of dry mustard
6 oz Cheddar cheese (grated)
4 gherkins
2 tomatoes (sliced)

1 Cut the avocado pears in half lengthwise. Remove stones and discard.

2 Place oil, vinegar, salt, pepper and mustard into a screw-top jar. Shake vigorously to mix thoroughly.

3 Place cheese in a basin, add the salad dressing. Mix thoroughly, then spoon on top of avocado pears.

4 Place pears on a shallow serving dish. Garnish each with a gherkin fan and sliced tomatoes.

French Picnic Loaf

Serves 4

$1\frac{1}{2}$ oz butter
$\frac{1}{2}$ oz flour
$\frac{1}{4}$ pint milk
4 oz Cheddar cheese (grated)
4 oz cooked chicken (chopped)
Salt and pepper
Parsley (chopped)
1 French loaf
2 eggs (hard-boiled and sliced)
2 tomatoes (sliced)

1 Place $\frac{1}{2}$ oz butter, flour and milk in a saucepan. Heat, whisking continuously, until the sauce thickens.

2 Add cheese, chicken, salt, pepper and parsley. Allow filling to become cold.

3 Make a deep slit along one complete side of the French loaf. Lightly butter bread.

4 Place filling inside French loaf. Garnish with sliced hard-boiled eggs and tomatoes along the cut edge. Serve cold.

Tip: This is also a great party favourite, too!

1. Cheese Nest—Page 70
2. Welsh Eggs—Page 70
3. Farmhouse Omelette—Page 65

Farmhouse Omelette

Serves 4

1 oz butter
1 onion (chopped)
2 oz streaky bacon (chopped)
3 eggs
Salt and pepper
Pinch of dry mustard
$2\frac{1}{2}$ fl oz milk
4 oz peas (cooked)
2 tomatoes (chopped)
2 oz mushrooms (quartered and cooked)
4 oz Cheddar cheese (grated)

1 Melt butter in large frying pan. Add onion and bacon, then fry until soft.

2 Beat together eggs, salt, pepper, mustard and milk. Add to frying pan, then scatter on top the peas, tomatoes and mushrooms. Fry, lightly stirring with a fork, until set.

3 Sprinkle the cheese on top. Cut omelette into 4 wedges and serve immediately, accompanied by a tossed green salad.

Tip: An ideal quick snack to serve when unexpected guests arrive—you may use any left-over vegetables from the previous meal to add colour and flavour to this omelette.

Sausage Whirls

Serves 4

1 lb pork sausages (8)
6 oz Cheddar cheese
4 rashers streaky bacon
Chutney
Watercress

1 Preheat grill.

2 Slit sausages lengthwise. Cut cheese into 8 rectangles so that the length corresponds with that of the sausages. Place cheese inside sausage slits.

3 Stretch rashers of bacon with the back of a knife. Cut in half and wrap each half-rasher around each sausage, spiral fashion. Secure, if necessary, with a wooden cocktail stick.

4 Place under grill and cook slowly, turning frequently, until the sausages are cooked throughout, for about 15-20 minutes.

5 Serve hot, garnished with watercress. Serve with chutney.

Cheesey Jacket Potatoes

Serves 4

4 large potatoes
2 oz butter (melted)
6 oz Cheddar cheese (grated)
1 tablespoon chives (snipped)
Salt and pepper
Pinch of nutmeg

1 Preheat oven—mark 6. 400°F.
2 Scrub potatoes, then prick well with a fork.
Bake for 1-1½ hours or until soft.
3 Cut potatoes in half lengthwise, scoop out the
centre. Mash well in basin. Add melted butter,
4 oz grated cheese, chives, salt, pepper and nutmeg.
Beat thoroughly.
4 Pipe mixture back into potato shells. Sprinkle with
remaining cheese. Return to oven for 10-15 minutes
to heat through and brown the top. Serve hot.

Jacket Baked Potatoes are an excellent idea at
parties for all age groups. Here are some suggested
fillings:
Grated Cheddar cheese and cooked mushrooms.
Chopped, grilled or fried bacon and sliced
Cheddar cheese.
Chopped tomatoes and sliced Cheddar cheese.
Grated Cheddar cheese and pickle.

Savoury Stuffed Apples

Serves 4

$\frac{1}{2}$ oz butter
5 rashers streaky bacon
1 onion (finely chopped)
2 oz Cheddar cheese (finely grated)
4 cooking apples

1 Preheat oven—mark 4, 350°F.

2 Chop 1 rasher of bacon. Melt butter in a saucepan, add bacon and onion, then fry until cooked.
Add grated cheese.

3 Remove core from apples, then score around the middle. Pack stuffing into each cavity.

4 Stretch the remaining rashers of bacon. Roll up, and secure with a wooden cocktail stick or skewer.

5 Place apples, surrounded by bacon rolls, in an ovenproof dish. Bake for 30-35 minutes, depending upon the size of the apples.

6 Serve hot, topped with a bacon roll.

Mexican Toast

Serves 4

4 slices bread
2 oz butter
1 (7 oz) can sweetcorn
6 oz Cheddar cheese (grated)
Salt and pepper
2 tomatoes (sliced)
Parsley

1 Preheat grill.

2 Toast bread on both sides. Butter liberally.
Keep hot.

3 Heat sweetcorn in a saucepan. Drain well. Add grated cheese, salt and pepper. Spread mixture on to hot buttered toast.

4 Top with sliced tomatoes. Place under grill to melt the cheese. Serve hot, garnished with sprigs of parsley.

Cheese Nest

Serves 4

1 lb potatoes (peeled)
2 oz butter
2 tablespoons milk
Salt and pepper
2 small onions (cut into rings)
2 oz mushrooms (sliced)
4 oz peas (cooked)
4 oz Cheddar cheese

1 Preheat oven—mark 5, 375°F

2 Boil the potatoes until soft. Drain, then mash with 1 oz butter, milk, salt and pepper. Pipe into a nest shape in a round, shallow ovenproof dish.

3 Melt remaining butter in a pan. Fry onions for 2-3 minutes until soft. Add mushrooms and cook until tender. Add peas.

4 Spoon into centre of dish. Cut cheese into thick shavings and press into vegetables.

5 Bake for 15-20 minutes until potato browns and cheese is bubbly on the surface. Serve hot.

Welsh Eggs

Serves 4

6 oz Cheddar cheese (grated)
1 lb potatoes (cooked and mashed)
$1\frac{1}{2}$ oz flour
Salt and pepper
4 eggs (hard-boiled)
1 egg (beaten)
Breadcrumbs
Deep fat for frying

1 Mix together the cheese, potatoes, flour, salt and pepper. Divide the mixture into four, then mould around each hard-boiled egg.

2 Brush each egg with beaten egg. Roll in breadcrumbs. Repeat this process once more.

3 Fry in hot, deep fat until golden and crisp. Drain thoroughly. Serve either hot with vegetables or cold with salad.

Quick Chick Tartlets

Makes 24

Shortcrust pastry using 8 oz plain flour
4 oz Cheddar cheese (finely grated)
6 oz cooked chicken (finely chopped)
2 sticks celery (chopped)
5 tablespoons mayonnaise
Salt and pepper

1 Preheat oven—mark 5, 375°F.

2 Roll out shortcrust pastry thinly. Cut 24 circles and use to line patty tins.

3 Mix together cheese, chicken, celery, mayonnaise, salt and pepper. Divide mixture between the patty tins.

4 Bake for 30 minutes. Serve hot or cold.

Tip: These Tartlets are really delicious. A quick and tasty way of using up cold chicken. They are a must for picnics and packed meals!

Cheese Soufflé

Serves 4

1 oz butter
1 oz flour
$\frac{1}{4}$ pint milk
3 eggs (separated)
Salt and pepper
$\frac{1}{2}$ level teaspoon mustard powder
4 oz Cheddar cheese (grated)

1 Preheat oven—mark 5, 375°F.

2 Place the butter, flour and milk in a saucepan. Heat, whisking continuously, until the sauce thickens. Remove from heat.

3 Whisk egg whites until stiff.

4 Beat the egg yolks, salt, pepper, mustard and cheese into sauce. Carefully fold in the whisked whites until well blended.

5 Turn mixture into a buttered 2-pint soufflé dish. Bake for 20-25 minutes until well risen. Serve immediately.

Toasted Cheese Club Sandwiches

Serves 4

3 oz butter
4 rashers streaky bacon (chopped)
4 oz mushrooms (sliced)
8 slices bread
2 tablespoons chutney
4 oz Cheddar cheese (sliced)
1 tomato (sliced)
Parsley

1 Preheat grill.
2 Melt $\frac{1}{2}$ oz butter in a saucepan. Add bacon and mushrooms, then fry until cooked.
3 Butter slices of bread. Make up sandwiches using bacon, mushrooms and chutney. Toast lightly on one side. Turn sandwiches over.
4 Top each sandwich with slices of cheese. Garnish with tomato. Return to grill to brown.
5 Serve hot, topped with parsley.

Tip: You may vary the filling ingredients to make other Toasted Club Sandwiches.

Toasted Cheese

For each serving, toast a slice of bread on one side—lay thinly sliced Cheddar cheese on the untoasted side and grill until golden brown.

There are many ways of garnishing toasted cheese. Here are some suggestions for suitable toppings:

Tomato slices
Mushrooms, lightly fried in butter
Poached egg
Fruit—apples, pineapple, oranges, etc
Sardines
Tuna fish
Stick of celery
Ham
Pickled onions
Gherkins
Olives
Pickles
Red cabbage
Watercress
Cucumber slices
Spring onions
Bacon rashers, grilled
Anchovy fillets
Rings of red or green peppers
Mandarin oranges
Chopped nuts
Raisins

Welsh Rarebit

Serves 4

Welsh Rarebit is perhaps one of our most famous cheese dishes. The true Welsh Rarebit is something a little more than toasted cheese. It is, in fact, a sauce and here is one method of preparing it. For an extra 'kick', try adding beer instead of milk.

1 oz butter
6 oz Cheddar cheese (grated)
$2\frac{1}{2}$ fl oz milk
Few drops Worcestershire sauce
1 teaspoon made mustard
Salt and pepper
4 large slices bread

1 Preheat grill.
2 Place butter, cheese, milk, Worcestershire sauce, mustard, salt and pepper in a saucepan.
3 Heat very gently until the sauce is thick and smooth.
4 Toast bread on one side only. Pour mixture over untoasted side and return to grill to brown. Serve hot.

Cheesey Squares

Serves 4

4 oz butter
4 slices bread
6 oz Cheddar cheese (sliced)
2 eggs (beaten)
Salt and pepper
Dry mustard
4 rashers bacon
2 tomatoes (halved)

1 Spread slices of bread with 2 oz of the butter. Using slices of cheese, make up cheese sandwiches. Cut each sandwich into 4 squares.

2 Beat together eggs, salt, pepper and mustard, in a shallow dish. Dip each sandwich in the seasoned egg to thoroughly coat.

3 Melt remaining butter in a frying pan. Fry the Cheesey Squares for about 5 minutes on each side, until golden and crispy on the outside. Drain well and keep hot.

4 Fry bacon and tomatoes until cooked. Serve with Cheesey Squares.

Tip: Nice for breakfast, too! An excellent way to use up cheese sandwiches after a party or picnic.

SWEETS

Almond Cheesecake

Serves 6–8

4 oz butter
1 oz soft brown sugar
8 dessertspoons golden syrup
6 oz digestive biscuits (crushed)
2 oz blanched almonds (chopped)
3 fl oz fresh double cream
6 oz Cheddar cheese (finely grated)
1 teaspoon lemon juice
2 oz caster sugar

1 Grease a 7-inch flan ring.

2 Melt together the butter, soft brown sugar and syrup in a saucepan, then stir in crushed biscuits. Mix thoroughly, then press into the prepared tin to form a base. Allow to set.

3 Sprinkle with 1 oz chopped almonds. Toast the remainder until golden brown.

4 Lightly whip the cream and add grated cheese, lemon juice and caster sugar. Spread over prepared base. Leave in a cool place to become firm, then serve, cut into wedges.

Cheese and Walnut Loaf

Serves 8

8 oz self-raising flour
1 level teaspoon salt
6 oz butter
4 oz Cheddar cheese (finely grated)
2 oz walnuts (chopped)
2 eggs (beaten)
$\frac{1}{4}$ pint milk

1 Preheat oven—mark 5, 375°F and butter a 1-lb loaf tin.
2 Sieve the flour and salt together into a bowl.
Rub in 4 oz butter until it resembles fine breadcrumbs.
Stir in cheese, walnuts, eggs and milk. Beat thoroughly.
3 Place mixture into the prepared loaf tin. Smooth the top
level. Bake for 50-55 minutes, until firm to the touch.
4 Cool and serve, cut in slices, thickly buttered.

Crispy Apple Flan

Serves 6

8 oz plain flour
$\frac{1}{4}$ level teaspoon salt
4 oz butter
2 level teaspoons caster sugar
5 tablespoons milk
1 oz soft brown sugar
1 oz cornflakes
1 oz sultanas
8 oz cooking apples (peeled, cored and thinly sliced)
2 oz Cheddar cheese (grated)

1 Preheat oven—mark 6, 400°F

2 Sieve together 6 oz flour and salt into a bowl. Rub in
3 oz butter until it resembles fine breadcrumbs. Stir in
caster sugar and 3 tablespoons milk, to make a stiff dough.
3 Roll out pastry to line an 8-inch pie plate.
4 Sieve remaining flour into a bowl. Rub in
remaining butter until it resembles fine breadcrumbs
then add brown sugar, cornflakes, sultanas,
apples, cheese and remaining milk. Mix thoroughly.
5 Place apple mixture on to prepared plate. Smooth
the top level. Bake for 30 minutes. Serve cold.

Cheesecake Wedges

Makes 16

6 oz butter
4 oz caster sugar
2 eggs (beaten)
4 oz self-raising flour
2 tablespoons milk
Pinch of salt
6 oz Cheddar cheese (finely grated)
2 oz stem ginger in syrup
2 oz walnut halves
2 rings pineapple (cut into wedges)

1 Preheat oven—mark 5, 375°F.

2 Grease two 7-inch sandwich tins.

3 Cream together the butter and sugar until light and fluffy. Beat in the eggs and a little of the flour, then the milk.

4 Combine remaining flour, salt and 4 oz grated cheese, then fold carefully into the creamed mixture.

5 Divide mixture between the prepared tins and smooth the tops level.

6 Bake for 20-25 minutes. Sprinkle with remaining grated cheese, then cool.

7 Cut into wedges then decorate with ginger, walnut halves and pineapple pieces. Serve.

Somerset Cake

Serves 6–8

8 oz butter (softened)
4½ oz caster sugar
2 eggs (beaten)
4 tablespoons milk
4 oz self-raising flour
Pinch of salt
2 teaspoons baking powder
2 tablespoons raspberry jam
6 oz Cheddar cheese (grated)
½ lemon (grated rind and juice)

1 Preheat oven—mark 5, 375°F.

2 Grease and line with greaseproof paper, two 7-inch sandwich tins.

3 Place 4 oz butter, sugar, eggs, 2 tablespoons milk, flour, salt and baking powder into a bowl. Beat thoroughly, until mixture is a soft dropping consistency.

4 Divide mixture between the two prepared tins, smooth tops level. Bake for about 25 minutes, until pale golden brown. Cool.

5 Spread raspberry jam on the top of one sponge.

6 Beat together remaining butter, cheese, milk and lemon juice until soft. Spread half of this filling on to other sponge. Place them together. Top with remaining cheese filling and mark the surface with a fork. Scatter grated lemon rind over the top.
Serve, cut into wedges.

Apple and Cheese Crumble

Serves 4

$1\frac{1}{2}$ lb cooking apples (peeled, cored and sliced)
6 oz Cheddar cheese (grated)
$\frac{1}{4}$ teaspoon cinnamon
2 oz soft brown sugar
2 oz raisins
6 oz plain flour
3 oz butter
2 oz caster sugar
5 fl oz fresh cream

1 Preheat oven—mark 6, 400°F.

2 Butter a 1-pint ovenproof pie dish. Place layers of apple slices, 4 oz cheese, cinnamon, soft brown sugar and raisins in the dish until all ingredients are used.

3 Sieve the flour into a bowl. Rub in the butter until it resembles fine breadcrumbs, stir in caster sugar and remaining cheese. Mix thoroughly.

4 Sprinkle crumble over apple layers. Bake for approximately 30-40 minutes until the top is crisp and golden.

5 Serve hot, with fresh cream.

Cheddar Cheesecake

Serves 6–8

5 oz self-raising flour
1 oz icing sugar
2½ oz butter
2 eggs (separated)
2 tablespoons milk
6 oz Cheddar cheese (grated)
2½ fl oz natural yogurt
1 lemon (grated rind and juice)
3 oz caster sugar

1 Preheat oven—mark 7, 425°F.

2 Sieve together 4 oz flour and icing sugar into a
bowl. Rub in the butter until it resembles fine
breadcrumbs. Mix to a stiff dough with 1 egg yolk
and milk.

3 Roll out pastry and use to line an 8-inch sandwich
tin or flan ring. Prick the base well. Bake 'blind'
for 10 minutes.

4 Mix together grated cheese, remaining egg yolk,
yogurt, remaining flour, lemon rind and juice, and
caster sugar. Beat well.

5 Whisk egg whites until light and fluffy. Fold
carefully into the cheese mixture. Pour into baked
flan case.

6 Reduce oven to mark 3, 325°F. Bake cheesecake
for a further 40-50 minutes, until firm and golden.
Serve cold.

Lemon Cheese Tarts

Makes 36

6 oz plain flour
Pinch of salt
3 oz butter
2 level teaspoons caster sugar
3 tablespoons milk
1 egg (beaten)
1 (5 fl oz) carton natural yogurt
1 oz granulated sugar
1 lemon (grated rind and juice)
6 oz Cheddar cheese (finely grated)

1 Preheat oven—mark 5, 375°F.
2 Sieve the flour and salt together into a bowl.
Rub in the butter until it resembles fine breadcrumbs.
Stir in caster sugar and milk, to form a stiff dough.
3 Roll out pastry thinly, then cut into rounds using
a 2½-inch cutter. Use to line 36 patty tins.
4 Beat together egg, yogurt, granulated sugar, lemon
rind and juice, and cheese. Divide mixture between
pastry cases.
5 Bake for 20-25 minutes, until golden brown.
Cool and serve.

Tip: This filling mixture is ideal in pancakes.

CHEESE AND PARTIES

1. Cheese Biscuits—Page 87
2. Indienne Cheese Balls—Page 87
3. Crunchy Cheese Bobs—Page 88
4. Cheese Bites—Page 88
5. Cheese Straws—Page 87

Cheese and Parties

Giving a party is fun, and Cheddar cheese can help solve the problem of what to serve. If you are having friends in for a meal, there are plenty of hot and cold ideas to use. If it's a snack party, choose a cheese and wine party. Go Continental, have a fondue party and let your guests dip into a delicious home-made fondue, or give your party an American touch with dips which are easy to serve. Alternatively, a simple, inexpensive and enjoyable way of entertaining is to offer a cheeseboard with wedges of a variety of cheeses, dishes of butter, a bowl of juicy apples, crusty loaves, biscuits or brown bread. For pre-lunch or early evening parties, serve different types of cheese cubed and speared with cocktail sticks. Whatever party you choose, you'll find cheese fits all occasions.

Here are some suggestions for suitable partners and garnishes to cheese:
Leicester—pineapple pieces, alone or rolled in a slice of ham
Lancashire—green grapes
Wensleydale—sliced apple
Cheddar—pickled onions
Derby—gherkins
Caerphilly—stuffed olives
Double Gloucester—black grapes
Cheshire—blanched carrot

How much to buy

Cheese—allow about 3 oz of cheese per head, but over-estimate rather than under-estimate your guests' capacity, remembering that cheese is very easy to store and use later.

Accompaniments—fruit and vegetables make a colourful, appetising display, serve rosy-red apples, grapes and crisp salad vegetables. Also serve a variety of plain biscuits, bread rolls, oatcakes, crusty bread, Melba toast, digestive biscuits, cream crackers and crispbreads. These, too, are easy to use up if they are not all required. Butter—if rolls or bread are included, allow 8 oz of butter for every 10 guests.

Cheese and Wine Parties

Cheese and wine parties have two special advantages—they are easy to run and they can be as formal or as impromptu as you wish. They are ideal if you want to relax and have a good party without too much hard work, and may be in or out of doors.

Here are suggestions for a spur-of-the-moment cheese and wine party which needs only those two ingredients and one or two other simple dishes. Then there are suggestions for a larger, more sophisticated cheese and wine party, where a buffet is served.

Cheese can be served in so many different ways.

Serve cheese:

1 In wedges—leaving guests to help themselves.
2 In diced cubes that can be speared with a cocktail stick or picked up and eaten with biscuits.

3 As a fondue
4 As a dip

} Serve with fingers of toast, biscuits, sticks of celery or sausages on sticks, all of which can be dunked into the cheese mixture.

Whatever the occasion, formal or informal, these ideas are easy to prepare, yet are bound to be winners.

Wine—be generous in your estimate of the quantity of wine: a good half-bottle for each guest. Never allow the party to run dry, your wine merchant will usually take back unopened bottles.

Party Pyramids

Makes 10

1 large sliced loaf
2 oz butter
4 tomatoes (sliced)
4 hard-boiled eggs (sliced)
4 oz prawns
2 carrots (finely grated)
Sliced raw button mushrooms
10 oz Cheddar cheese
Celery (chopped)
Gherkins
Parsley

1 Cut 10 circles, of each size, from the sliced bread, using a 4-inch, 3-inch, 2-inch, 1½-inch and 1-inch cutter. Butter each circle liberally.

2 Assemble circles of bread in pyramid fashion with any of the suggested ingredients. Use a layer of either grated or sliced cheese in each.

3 Garnish with gherkins or parsley. Serve.

Indienne Cheese Balls

Makes 24

8 oz Cheddar cheese (finely grated)
4 level tablespoons chutney
1 level teaspoon curry powder
2 oz whole blanched almonds
2 oz almonds (finely chopped)

1 Place cheese in a basin. Add chutney and curry powder. Mix to a firm paste.
2 Roll small quantities of cheese mixture round each almond. Roll each ball firmly in the chopped almonds. Serve.

Tip: In place of whole almonds, place stuffed olives in the centre.

Cheese Biscuits and Straws

4 oz plain flour
$\frac{1}{2}$ teaspoon salt
Pinch dry mustard
3 oz butter
3 oz Cheddar cheese (grated)
1 egg (beaten)

1 Preheat oven—mark 6, 400°F.
2 Sieve together flour, salt and mustard into a basin. Rub in butter until the mixture resembles fine breadcrumbs. Stir in the cheese.
3 Bind ingredients together with beaten egg. Knead lightly.
4 Roll out on a floured board to $\frac{1}{8}$ inch thickness and cut into circles, shapes, or narrow strips for cheese straws.
5 Bake for approximately 10-15 minutes, until golden brown. Serve hot or cold.

Crunchy Cheese Bobs

Makes approximately 24

3 oz butter
6 oz Cheddar cheese (grated)
Pinch of dry mustard
Salt and pepper
2 (small) packets potato crisps (crushed)

1 Soften the butter in a basin. Beat in the cheese, mustard, salt and pepper.
2 Form mixture into balls, then roll in crushed potato crisps. Chill and serve on sticks.

Cheese Spears

Make small spears by placing cubes of Cheddar cheese on cocktail sticks with any one or a selection of the following:

Prawns
Tomato quarters
Cocktail onions
Stuffed olives
Gherkins

Apple cubes
   (dipped in lemon juice)
Grilled bacon rolls
Salami rolls
Pineapple cubes
Green or black grapes

These spears make an eye-catching centrepiece if you stick all of them into one of the following bases:

Small French loaf
Small loaves
Oranges
Grapefruit
Firm cabbage
Half cucumber

Fresh pineapple
Cob loaf
Large potato
Marrow
Melon

Cheese Bites

Dice Cheddar cheese into small cubes and toss in celery salt.

Toss cubes with walnuts and serve in a bowl for people to help themselves.

Open Sandwiches

Open sandwiches are ideal for parties of all kinds; they are also good for packed meals.

Brown or wholemeal bread makes an interesting base. Make the toppings as decorative and colourful as possible.

Toppings:

Lettuce, grated Cheddar cheese, grated carrot and pickle.

Lettuce, grated Cheddar cheese, sliced tomato and pickle.

Lettuce, grated Cheddar cheese, sliced hard-boiled egg, sliced tomato and mayonnaise.

Lettuce, sliced Cheddar cheese, slice of ham and pickle.

Lettuce, sliced Cheddar cheese, sliced hard-boiled egg and pickle.

Lettuce, cubed Cheddar cheese and sliced tomato.

Lettuce, cubed Cheddar cheese and pineapple chunks.

Lettuce, cubed Cheddar cheese, hard-boiled egg and mayonnaise.

French Loaf

Long French loaves, when filled with salad ingredients, can look most attractive. They can be called crocodiles for children's parties! Cut into 3-inch to 4-inch lengths for serving.

Fillings:

Grated Cheddar cheese, lettuce, tomato and cucumber.

Grated Cheddar cheese, grated carrot and pickle.

Grated Cheddar cheese, hard-boiled egg, mayonnaise and lettuce.

Grated Cheddar cheese, lettuce, chopped apple, chopped celery and mayonnaise.

Grated Cheddar cheese, lettuce and baked beans.

Cheddar Mille Feuille

Serves 4–6

1 (16 oz) packet frozen puff pastry (thawed)
4 oz butter
6 oz Cheddar cheese (grated)
2 tablespoons fresh cream
Salt and pepper
Cayenne pepper
Pinch dry mustard
Stuffed olives (sliced)
Gherkins (sliced)

1 Preheat oven—mark 8, 450°F.

2 Roll out pastry to a rectangle of 9 inches by 12 inches.
Divide into 3 strips, 9 inches by 4 inches.
Place on a wetted baking tray. Prick well
with a fork, then bake for 15-20 minutes. Cool.

3 Cream together the butter and cheese. Add fresh
cream, salt, pepper and mustard. Beat thoroughly
until soft.

4 Trim strips of pastry. Spread one-third of the
cheese filling on to each strip. Sandwich together.
Crush pastry trimmings finely and use to decorate the
top, together with sliced olives and gherkins.
Serve chilled.

Cheese Grills

Makes 28

8 oz Cheddar cheese (grated)
1 level tablespoon tomato ketchup
1 level tablespoon mayonnaise
28 small biscuits

1 Preheat grill.

2 Mix together cheese, tomato ketchup and
mayonnaise. Spread thickly on the small biscuits.

3 Toast under a hot grill for a few minutes. Serve cold.

Toasted Sandwiches

Make up sandwiches in the normal way and toast briskly on both sides before serving.

Some suggested fillings:

Grated Cheddar cheese, chutney and tomato slices.

Grated Cheddar cheese and onion rings.

Grated Cheddar cheese and scrambled egg.

Grated Cheddar cheese, scrambled egg and tomato slices.

Grated Cheddar cheese, scrambled egg and chopped cooked bacon.

Grated Cheddar cheese, scrambled egg, mayonnaise and watercress.

Cheese and Tomato Whirls

Makes 16

8 oz self-raising flour
2 oz butter
$\frac{1}{2}$ teaspoon dry mustard
4 oz Cheddar cheese (grated)
Salt and pepper
4 tablespoons milk
1 egg (beaten)
2-3 tablespoons tomato purée

1 Preheat oven—mark 7, 425°F.

2 Sift flour into a bowl. Rub in butter until the mixture resembles fine breadcrumbs. Add mustard, 2 oz cheese, salt and pepper, then mix well.

3 Add enough milk and egg and bind to form a soft dough. Roll out to an oblong of approximately 14 inches by 7 inches. Spread with tomato purée, then sprinkle with remaining cheese.

4 Roll up dough, Swiss roll fashion, starting from the longest side. Moisten the edge to secure well, with a little milk. Cut into 16 portions $\frac{1}{2}$ inch wide.

5 Place whirls, cut side down, on well buttered baking trays. Bake for 15-20 minutes, until golden brown. Serve hot.

Peanut Butter Biscuits

Makes 36

6 oz self-raising flour
Pinch of salt
1 oz butter
2 oz peanut butter
4 oz Cheddar cheese (grated)
1 egg (beaten)
Milk
1 oz peanuts (chopped)

1 Preheat oven—mark 6, 400°F.

2 Sieve together flour and salt into a basin. Rub in the butter and peanut butter until the mixture resembles fine breadcrumbs. Add cheese and mix well.

3 Add egg and sufficient milk to bind mixture to make a firm dough.

4 Roll out dough to $\frac{1}{4}$ inch in thickness and cut into 36 fingers with a knife. Place on a baking tray, brush with milk and sprinkle with peanuts.

5 Bake for 15 minutes, until well risen, golden brown and firm.

Apple and Cheese Rolls

Makes 4

4 bridge rolls
2 oz butter
1 cooking apple
4 oz Cheddar cheese (grated)
4 tablespoons mayonnaise
Salt and pepper
Mustard and cress

1 Split rolls down the centre, but do not cut right through. Remove the soft bread and crumble. Spread rolls with butter.

2 Chop the apple and place in a basin. Add the cheese, bread, mayonnaise, salt and pepper. Mix well.

3 Place filling into the rolls. Close firmly and garnish with mustard and cress.

Party Dips

Why not try a dip? They are always popular at parties and look so attractive. Serve small biscuits, carrots, celery sticks, gherkins, cauliflower sprigs, cubes of French bread, radishes and potato crisps for dunking into dips.

Here is the basic recipe—simply vary the dips by adding one of the ingredients suggested for the Potted Cheese Spread.

Cheese Dip

6 oz Cheddar cheese (grated)
1 (5 fl oz) carton natural yogurt
2 tablespoons mayonnaise
Salt
Paprika pepper
Watercress

1 Beat together cheese, yogurt and mayonnaise. Add salt, then pile into a small dish and sprinkle with paprika pepper.
2 Garnish with watercress. Serve, surrounded by any of the suggestions for party dips.

Potted Cheese Spread

4 oz butter
Salt and pepper
$\frac{1}{2}$ teaspoon made mustard
8 oz Cheddar cheese (grated)
Few drops Worcestershire sauce
3–4 tablespoons milk

1 Cream butter well, then add salt, pepper, mustard, cheese and Worcestershire sauce. Beat in milk to make a smooth spread. Chill.
2 Spread on toast or bread.

This mixture can also be shaped into a neat sausage and coated with ground almonds and cut into slices.

Variations of Potted Cheese Spread

This spread will keep well for a few days in a screw-top jar or plastic container either in the refrigerator or a cool place. It is well worthwhile making a large enough quantity for several days' use.

A variety of additional flavourings can be added to the basic recipe at the time of use. Some suggestions include:

Horseradish sauce
Tomatoes (chopped)
4 level tablespoons chutney or pickle
Chives (chopped)
Mixed herbs (chopped)
4 fl oz sherry
Nuts (chopped)
Raisins
Celery (chopped)
Gherkins (chopped)
Pickled onions
Anchovy essence
Cold, crisp bacon (chopped)
5 fl oz beer
Tomato purée
Walnuts (chopped)
Apple (chopped)
Vinegar

Hard-boiled eggs (chopped)
Green pepper (chopped)
1 teaspoon curry powder
3 level tablespoons mayonnaise

1 level teaspoon onion (grated)
12 stuffed olives (chopped)
1 level tablespoon tomato ketchup
Cucumber (chopped)
Worcestershire sauce
2 tablespoons powdered onion soup or an alternative flavour
6 oz packet frozen kipper fillets (cooked and flaked)
1 (7 oz) can tuna or salmon
Mustard
Parsley (chopped)
1 (8 oz) can pineapple (chopped)
Sweetcorn (drained)
Ham (chopped)
Dried onions